Pebble® Plus

Dogs, Dogs, Dogs

All about German Shepherds

by Erika L. Shores

Consulting Editor: Gail Saunders-Smith, PhD

CAPSTONE PRESS
a capstone imprint

Pebble Plus is published by Capstone Press,
1710 Roe Crest Drive, North Mankato, Minnesota 56003.
www.capstonepub.com

Library of Congress Cataloging-in-Publication Data
Shores, Erika L., 1976–
All about German shepherds / by Erika L. Shores.
p. cm.—(Pebble plus. Dogs, dogs, dogs)
Includes bibliographical references and index.
Summary: "Full-color photographs and simple text provide a brief introduction to German shepherds"—Provided by
publisher.
ISBN 978-1-4296-8725-6 (library binding)
ISBN 978-1-62065-293-0 (ebook PDF)
1. German shepherd dog—Juvenile literature. I. Title.
SF429.G37S54 2013
636.737'6—dc23   2011049819

Editorial Credits
Juliette Peters, designer; Marcie Spence, media researcher; Kathy McColley, production specialist

Photo Credits
Alamy: Junior Bildarchiv, 7; Capstone Studio: Karon Dubke, 5, 11, 13; Fiona Green: 1, 3, 19; Shutterstock:
Luna Vandoorne, 21, Monika Wisniewska, 17, Natalia_Ostapenko, cover, s-eyerkaufer, 9, Svetlana Valoueva, 15

Note to Parents and Teachers

The Dogs, Dogs, Dogs series supports national science standards related to life science.
This book describes and illustrates German shepherds. The images support early readers in
understanding the text. The repetition of words and phrases helps early readers learn new
words. This book also introduces early readers to subject-specific vocabulary words, which are
defined in the Glossary section. Early readers may need assistance to read some words and to
use the Table of Contents, Glossary, Read More, Internet Sites, and Index sections of the book.

Printed in the United States of America in North Mankato, Minnesota.
042013   007246R

Table of Contents

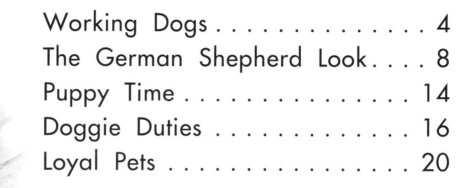

Working Dogs

German shepherds are working dogs.

They work with the police

to sniff out drugs and criminals.

German shepherds help find

missing people too.

German shepherds sometimes work as guide dogs. They lead people who are blind safely along streets. While working, guide dogs wear a harness.

The German Shepherd Look

German shepherds are long
and lean. They are 22 to 26 inches
(56 to 66 centimeters) tall.
Shepherds weigh 55 to 95 pounds
(25 to 43 kilograms).

Most German shepherds have black and tan coats. The hair around a shepherd's neck is longer than the rest of its coat.

German shepherds have long faces like wolves. Shepherds can smell very well. They also have a good sense of hearing. Their big pointed ears stand upright.

Puppy Time

German shepherd puppies have floppy ears. Their ears stand up as they grow older. After 8 weeks, puppies can leave their mothers. Shepherds live up to 15 years.

Doggie Duties

Every dog needs a good owner
to care for it. Owners feed
German shepherds each day.
These active dogs
also need lots of water.

A German shepherd's thick coat sheds hair all the time. Owners should brush shepherds every day. Shepherds shed the most in spring.

Loyal Pets

German shepherds are
popular pets.
People enjoy these smart,
loyal, and active dogs.

Glossary

active—being busy and moving around

coat—an animal's hair or fur

criminal—someone who commits a crime

guide dog—a dog that is trained to lead a person who is blind

harness—a set of straps attached to something else; a person who is blind holds on to part of a harness worn by a guide dog

lean—having little or no fat

loyal—being true to something or someone

popular—enjoyed or liked by many

sense—a way of knowing about your surroundings; German shepherds have excellent senses of seeing, smelling, and hearing

shed—to drop or fall off

Read More

Beal, Abigail. *I Love My German Shepherd.* Top Dogs. New York: PowerKids Press, 2011.

Lunis, Natalie. *German Shepherd: Super Smart.* Big Dogs Rule. New York: Bearport Pub., 2012.

Schuh, Mari. *German Shepherds.* Dog Breeds. Minneapolis: Bellwether Media, 2009.

Internet Sites

FactHound offers a safe, fun way to find Internet sites related to this book. All of the sites on FactHound have been researched by our staff.

Here's all you do:

Visit *www.facthound.com*

Type in this code: 9781429687256

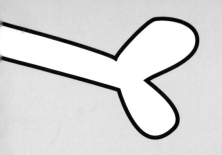

Index

Word Count: 208
Grade: 1
Early-Intervention Level: 15